BIG
BEASTS
Snake

Stephanie Turnbull

Published by Smart Apple Media,
an imprint of Black Rabbit Books
P.O. Box 3263, Mankato, Minnesota, 56002
www.blackrabbitbooks.com

Designed by Hel James
Edited by Mary-Jane Wilkins

Library of Congress Cataloging-in-Publication Data
Turnbull, Stephanie.
  Snake / Stephanie Turnbull.
    pages cm. -- (Big beasts)
  Summary: "Describes the characteristics of Snakes
and their life and habitat"-- Provided by publisher.
  Audience: Grades K to 3.
  Includes index.
  ISBN 978-1-77092-219-8 (paperback)
  1. Snakes--Juvenile literature. I. Title.
  QL666.O6T77 2015
  597.96--dc23
                              2014003974

CIP record is available from Library and Archives Canada

Photo acknowledgements
l = left, r = right, t = top, b = bottom
title page Vishnevskiy Vasily/Shutterstock; page 3 Ryan M. Bolton/
Shutterstock; 4 fivespots, 5 Patrick K. Campbell/both Shutterstock;
6 iStockphoto/Thinkstock; 7 Dan Exton/Shutterstock; 8-9 Stu
Porter/Shutterstock; 10 reptiles4all, 11 Robert Adrian Hillman/
both Shutterstock; 12 iStockphoto/Thinkstock; 13 lvalin/
Shutterstock; 14 Trahcus, 15 Alberto Loyo/both Shutterstock;
16 iStockphoto/Thinkstock; 17 Heiko Kiera/Shutterstock;
18 Tom Reichner/Shutterstock; 19 iStockphoto/Thinkstock;
20 Heiko Kiera, 21 Eric Isselee/both Shutterstock; 22t Catalin
Petolea, c Joyce Mar, 23 Matthew Cole/all Shutterstock
Cover Eric Isselee/Shutterstock

Printed in China

DAD0059
032014
9 8 7 6 5 4 3 2 1

Contents

Massive Monsters 4

Hot Homes 6

Big Eaters 8

On the Hunt 10

Lying in Wait 12

Crushing Coils 14

Deadly Bites 16

Stay Away! 18

Snake Babies 20

BIG Facts 22

Useful Words 24

Index 24

Some snakes are

colossal!

Massive Monsters

The **l o n g e s t** snake in the world is the reticulated python. These enormous beasts live deep in the thick forests of South-East Asia.

The **largest, *heaviest*** snake is the green anaconda of South America.

Hot Homes

Snakes live all over the world.
They are reptiles, so they like hot places
where they can bask in the **sun** to keep warm.

Their bodies are
covered in smooth,
overlapping scales.

Snakes are
great swimmers.
Many live in
steamy swamps
or tropical oceans.

Big Eaters

All snakes are meat-eaters.
They have flexible jaws that open
extra-wide!

This lets them gulp down lizards, bats, birds, fish, small snakes, and many other animals whole.

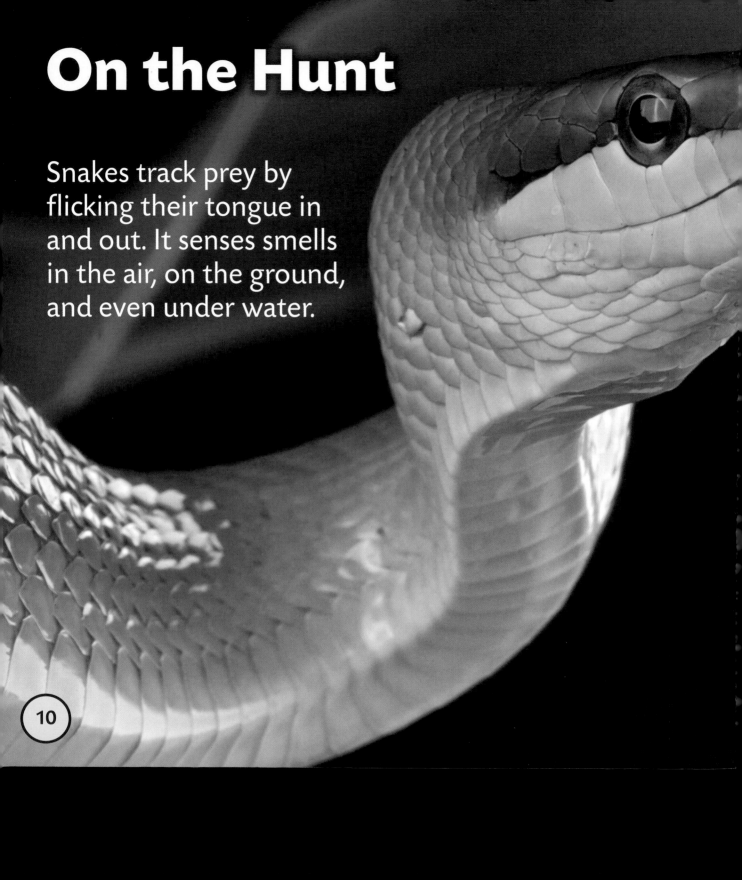

On the Hunt

Snakes track prey by flicking their tongue in and out. It senses smells in the air, on the ground, and even under water.

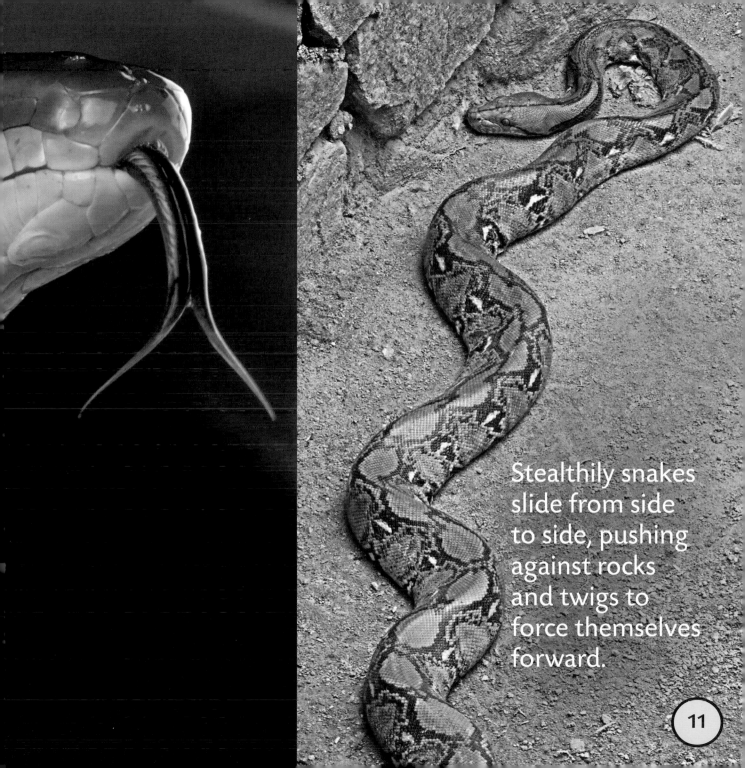

Stealthily snakes slide from side to side, pushing against rocks and twigs to force themselves forward.

Lying in Wait

When snakes spot prey, they hide
and wait for it to come close.

Patterned skin makes them
hard to spot among leaves or in trees.

Yellow eyelash vipers are the perfect color to hide in bunches of ripe bananas!

Crushing Coils

When anacondas, pythons, and boas catch prey, they wrap themselves around the animal... and *squeeeeeeze*.

The animal can't breathe and soon dies.

Enormous snakes such as this python can squeeze and kill animals as big as pigs, deer, and antelope!

Deadly Bites

Some snakes use poisonous liquid called venom to stun and kill prey.

As they lunge forward, hollow fangs spring out and **stab** their victim. Venom *squirts* through the fangs and deep into the animal.

Venomous snakes are often slim, with triangular heads, like this deadly green mamba.

Stay Away!

Snakes like to avoid humans. If they feel threatened, they warn people away with an angry *hisssss*.

A rattlesnake shakes the scaly segments at the end of its tail to make a loud rattle.